Montgomery County, Indiana
Through Time

William P. Helling

America Through Time®
Adding Color to American History

America Through Time is an imprint of Fonthill Media LLC
www.through-time.com
office@through-time.com

Published by Arcadia Publishing by arrangement with Fonthill Media LLC
For all general information, please contact Arcadia Publishing:
Telephone: 843-853-2070
Fax: 843-853-0044
E-mail: sales@arcadiapublishing.com
For customer service and orders:
Toll-Free 1-888-313-2665

www.arcadiapublishing.com

First published 2019

ISBN 978-1-63500-099-3

Typeset in Mrs Eaves XL Serif Narrow
Printed and bound in England

INTRODUCTION

Montgomery County, Indiana, was a densely wooded area that was inhabited by several Native American tribes and traversed by French hunters and trappers well before the arrival of the first American explorers in 1813. In that year, Major Ambrose Whitlock, Captain Williamson Dunn, and Lieutenant Henry Ristine noted the land along Sugar Creek as a possible settlement. The state of Indiana created Montgomery County in 1822, but settlers had already begun to investigate the region's possibilities. The first county election took place the next year, and by the end of 1824, land sales by auction conducted at the United States Land Office on North Water Street in Crawfordsville began to more quickly distribute many of the county's remaining tracts. It is not a particularly large county at just over 500 square miles, but it is rich in history and fortunate to have preserved many of its documents—if not its buildings—through the years. By 1830, the county population had grown to 7,317 people, and it doubled by the next census ten years later. Since that time, Montgomery County has had only a few years when the population did not increase, and the 2010 census counted 38,124 residents.

When I first arrived in Crawfordsville in 1986, I was confused when local citizens spoke of "townships." Even if this term should have been familiar to me, it was not, certainly owing to the lesser importance given to civil townships in the region where I grew up. These geographic and political subdivisions of a county, all identifiable by name, played an important role in the history of the county; each township is unique not only in resources but in population and services. In addition, until recently, the township system played a much larger role in local governance. But I soon learned that it was important to be aware of one's township and what it provided, even if I still had to look on a map in order to locate and even name the townships where I did not reside.

When I first proposed gathering materials for this book's topic, I was thinking mainly about using the resources of Crawfordsville, the county seat (population 15,915 at the 2010 census), which is by far the largest town in the county and the location of so much of its history. But I thought that concentration rather unfair, because I wanted to represent all of Montgomery County. Instead, I chose to look into each township for some of its special features. Some townships have fared better than others in retaining residents and preserving historic structures, but it is all worth noting, and no observation that I make should be considered a criticism. Finally, looking at the townships finally gave me a chance to acquaint myself with regions I had previously ignored. I am fortunate to have worked for the Crawfordsville District Public Library for nearly two decades, because this institution is the repository for so many of the county's artifacts, including the historic images that make up most of this work. The library is also in close cooperation with county residents outside of the town's limits who have shared with us so much of their private collections over the years.

I thus decided to organize this book of *Montgomery County Through Tim*e by township. The county has eleven townships, all encircling that which holds Crawfordsville. Each chapter will focus on one of the townships, beginning in the north-west corner of the county and proceeding clockwise around the outside: Coal Creek, Madison, Sugar Creek, Franklin, Walnut, Clark, Scott, Brown, Ripley, and Wayne. I then end with the central township, Union. Even when typing this list, I still had to refer to my notes to make sure I listed the townships correctly, and I am sure that I am not the only county resident ignorant in this aspect of Montgomery County geography. For this reason, I also start each chapter with a county map originally published in the 1876 *Illustrated Historical Atlas of the State of Indiana,* marked with the location of the township in question.

This book is not meant to be an historical overview, but I will refer interested readers to an entertaining if often tedious late-nineteenth century history of the county by Hiram W. Beckwith, *History of Montgomery County: together with historic notes on the Wabash Valley, gleaned from early authors, old maps and manuscripts, private and official correspondence, and other authentic, though, for the most part, out-of-the-way sources* (Chicago : H. H. Hill and N. Iddings, 1881). For county history beyond the publication of this old tome, the Crawfordsville District Public Library has no shortage of published and self-published works.

Each township has its fascinating local history and lore, but I cannot admit that each township shares equally in photographs or other documents that make an organizational effort like mine simple. To be fair, I chose three representative photographs or portrayals of each of the ten smaller townships, reserving the rest for the more populated Union township. Only I am aware of how many memorable images I had to leave out. Omissions of any favorite locales and content errors are all mine.

I hope you enjoy this trip around Montgomery County as much as I did creating it.

Contents

Acknowledgments

I could not nor would I want to attempt any worthwhile project such as this without the support of my family who tolerates so well my endless trivia about Montgomery County history—most of which could not fit into this book, of course. My wife, Jane, understands my need to undertake this task and encourages me; my children, John, Ryan, and Elizabeth support me in all I attempt. My father is a model for how hard I try to work; my mother instilled in me a love of learning that will never be extinguished.

My gratitude is extended particularly to Dellie Craig, my tireless colleague for twenty years at the Crawfordsville District Public Library. Dellie and I have labored together for so long and have moved a few inches the mountain of material we have taken responsibility for. If I need a photograph extricated from the archives or anything else associated with Montgomery County history, Dellie is always there for me.

A special thank you to Matthew Rodriguez, acquisitions editor for America Through Time, for suggesting this project and supporting my efforts. Matthew was always ready to help. And Kena Longabaugh, managing editor, was instrumental in prepping the manuscript.

I am also indebted to the Crawfordsville District Public Library (www.cdpl.lib.in.us) for its support over these many years. The library holds all the photographs and the rights to the images used in this book, whether in analog or digital form. We have always had a core collection, and it grows yearly thanks to donations from many interested parties from both near and far. Much of what the library holds is published and searchable online at: history.cdpl.lib.in.us

Please contact the Reference/Local History Department of the Crawfordsville District Public Library (ref@cdpl.lib.in.us, 765-362-2242 ext. 117) if you want historical information or if you can contribute to Montgomery County history with oral histories, family documents, letters, photographs, or ephemera. The library takes very seriously its commitment to preserve the heritage of Montgomery County, and we work closely with our museum department, the Carnegie Museum of Montgomery County (www.cdpl.lib.in.us/services/carnegie). The museum holds a large collection of county artifacts and deserves your visit.

You can do your part to help us preserve and enjoy what belongs to all of us.

1

Coal Creek Township

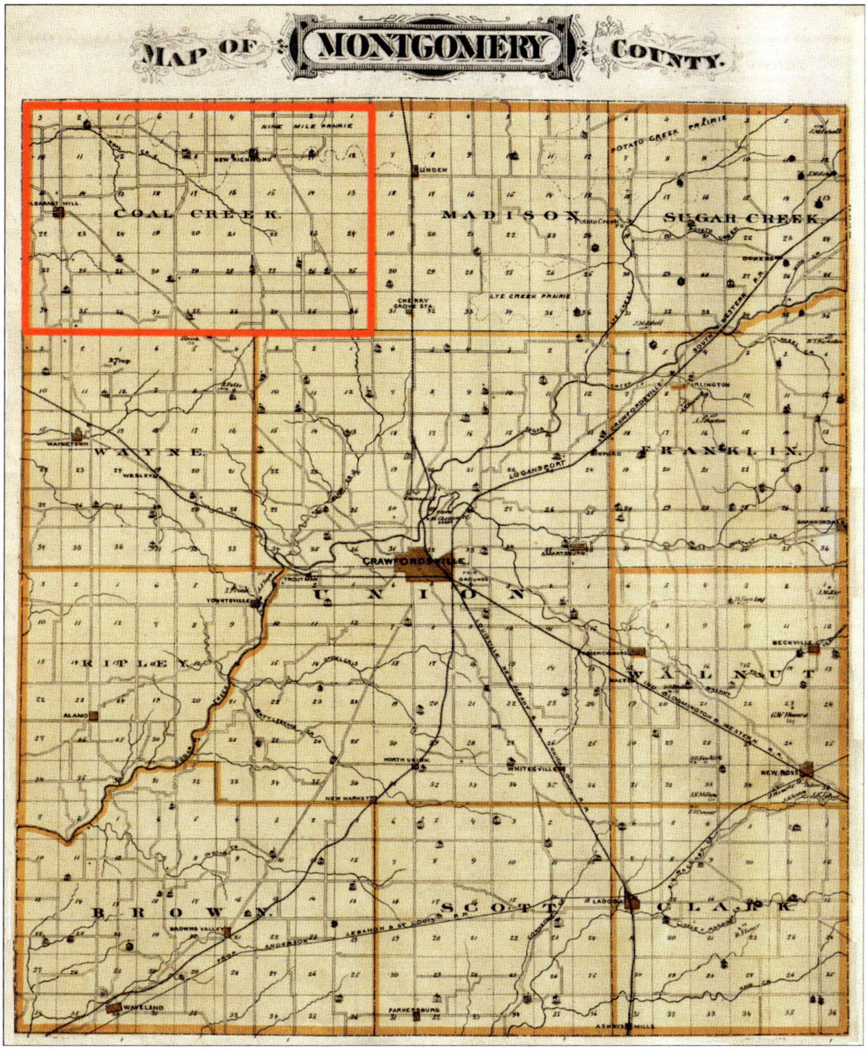

A creek that runs across the northern part of the township was named Coal Creek because of the coal found along its banks, and the name was eventually borrowed for the township. The first European settlers arrived in 1823 to an area reputed to be more grass and pasture than forest, and a popular hunting ground for the Native American inhabitants. New Richmond and Wingate are its towns, along with the unincorporated Elmdale.

NEW RICHMOND SCHOOLS: The first brick schoolhouse in New Richmond was erected in 1907; the first and second graders of that year posed proudly with their teacher in front of the structure. Four decades later, local children were attending the Coal Creek Central School—and still posing for their annual photograph with their teacher. By the end of the twentieth century, elementary students would be sent to the Pleasant Hill Elementary School.

WABASH STREET, NEW RICHMOND: The Knights of Pythias Hall was completed near the end of 1910 on the corner of Wabash Street, south of Washington Street. The hall stood next to Mason's Hardware & Furniture store, recognizable by its advertising painted on the side of the building. Town population was 464 in 1910, but it has declined by more than 100 at the time of writing.

VINE STREET, WINGATE: Wingate, platted in 1831, was formerly known as Pleasant Hill, but the name was changed around 1881 to honor J. C. Wingate, an elderly local citizen known for promoting the town. Downtown Wingate had several elegant structures on Vine Street around 1910, when the town had 446 residents. Wingate's current population was about half that amount at the 2010 census.

2

Madison Township

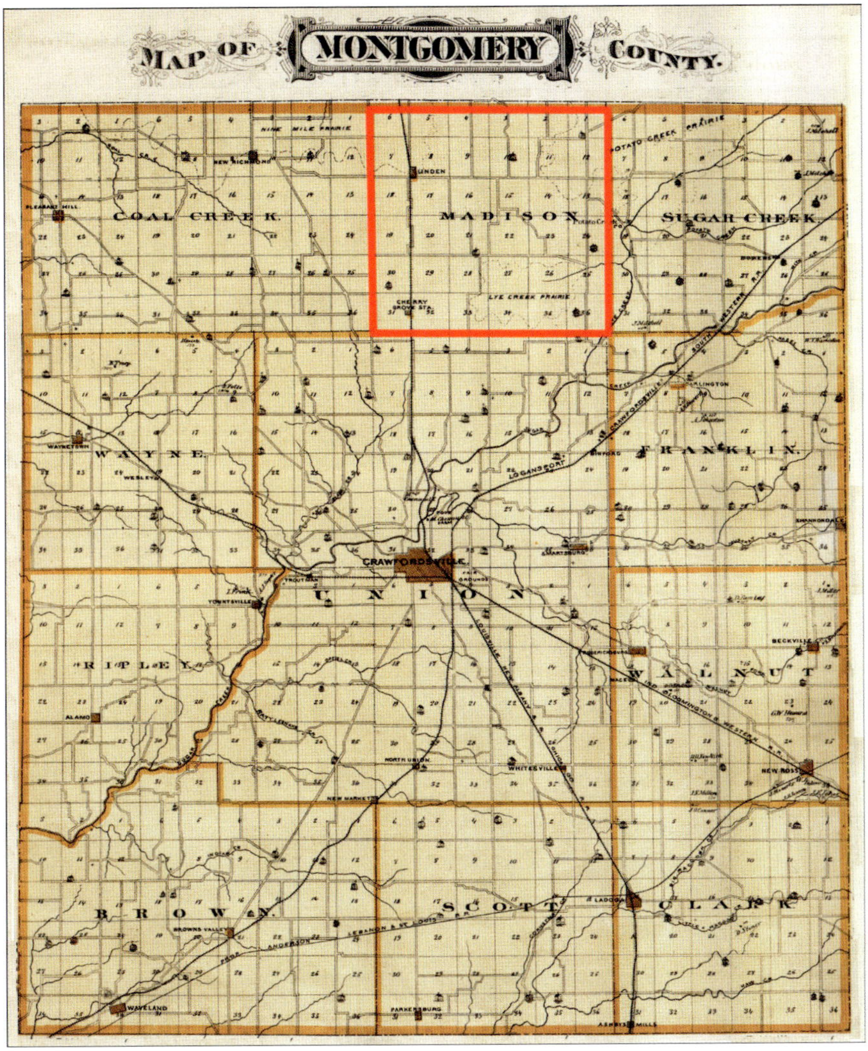

Madison Township was originally a marshy area whose largest swamp resembled a small lake. The first settlers arrived in 1829 and suffered many hardships before roads were constructed; ice in the winter and wet conditions at other times made travel difficult. There were no nearby mills, and local game often consumed the grain before it was harvested. Many smaller swamps and ponds made cultivation difficult before they were drained. Linden is the largest town; Cherry Grove and Kirkpatrick are unincorporated.

WALNUT STREET, LINDEN: Walnut Street was a tree-lined avenue around 1900. Linden had 572 residents at the time and was a slowly growing town. By the 2010 census, Linden was the home of 759 residents, its highest count over the past century. It is thought that the town was named for the many linden trees found in the area, and Walnut Street looking north is still a residential area. Surprisingly, there is no Linden Street.

UNLOADING GRAIN IN LINDEN: In 1865, a mill was located on the southeast corner of Main and Water streets in Linden, and was later converted to a grain elevator in 1890. In the first decades of the twentieth century, corn pickers would unload their haul on Main Street itself. This dirt road was paved in 1930 and widened in 1958 to become a busy U.S. 231 a few years later, on which few nowadays dare to linger.

KIRKPATRICK'S RISE AND FALL: Kirkpatrick was platted in 1882 to take advantage of the rail traffic rolling through the area. The area seemed destined for rapid growth. However, several railroad tank cars carrying gasoline derailed in 1917, igniting the fluid, and the town was greatly damaged. Visitors arrived for days to view the wreckage, and the town unfortunately never recovered. Kirkpatrick has shrunk to just a few structures, and all evidence of the railroad that ran through the area has long disappeared.

3

Sugar Creek Township

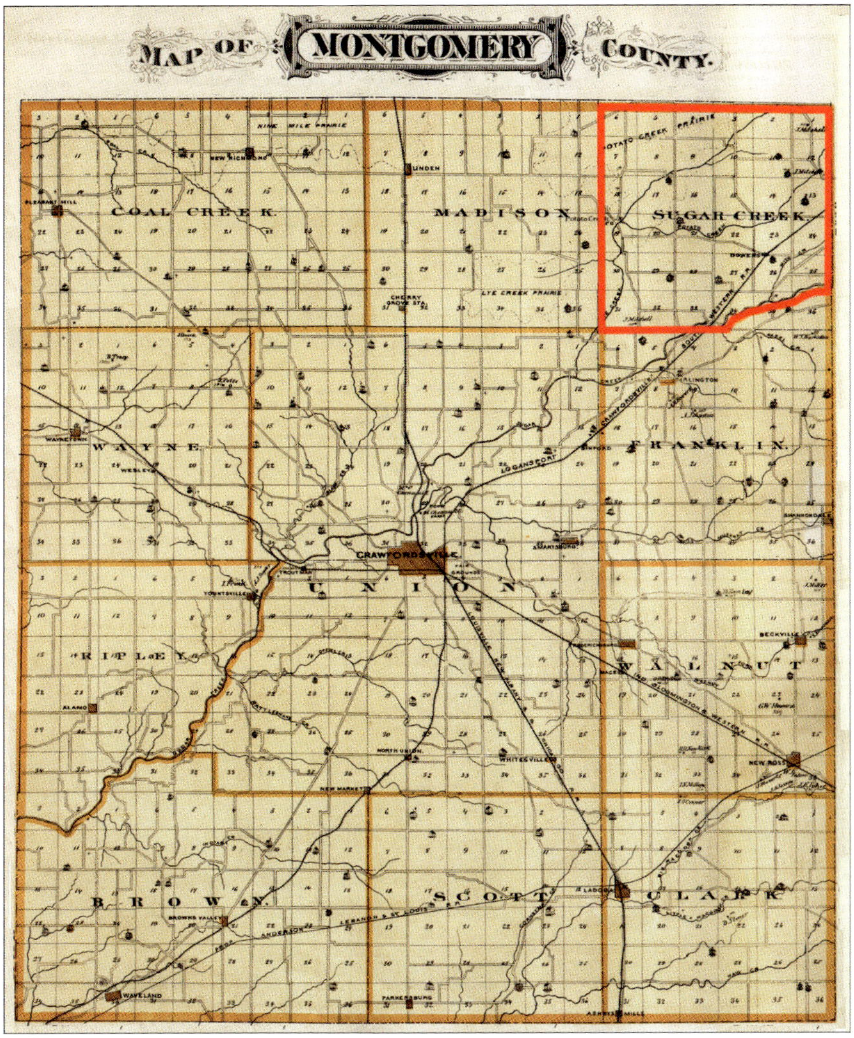

The first settlers in this area congregated around 1828 along the banks of Sugar Creek, which runs along the southeast portion of the township. In the early years of the township, residents were hopeful that Sugar Creek could be made more navigable so as to allow waterway shipping of wheat and corn all the way to New Orleans. But the arrival of the railroad by mid-century proved to be the only practical solution. Bowers is the only town; it is unincorporated. In 2010, the population of the township was 448, down from 903 reported in the 1910 census.

BERRYMAN FARM: An engraving in the 1878 *Montgomery County Atlas* shows the farm of Dr. James B. Berryman, near Potato Creek. Potato Creek runs southwest across the township; this portion was called Potato Creek Prairie because of the abundance of wild potatoes that grew there. Remnants of some later farm buildings remain on this land, however.

Bowers School Children: Many early residents of the township arrived from Ohio and brought with them a desire to educate their children well. It is recorded that 1833 actually saw the second schoolhouse built at what is now Bowers Station. The 1914 construction of Bowers School gave the area a fine structure, and it served until 1959, when declining numbers forced its closure. The building eventually became dilapidated and was demolished.

DUNKARD CHURCH: The German Baptists, known as the Dunkards, organized in 1856 in the township and met in houses of the members. A brick structure was eventually erected in 1893. The Dunkards grew from ten members to more than thirty by the early 1900s, but disappeared by the 1950s. The church would have been near the bend of 850 E and 1050 North, but is now gone, although Bowers Cemetery is still nearby.

4

Franklin Township

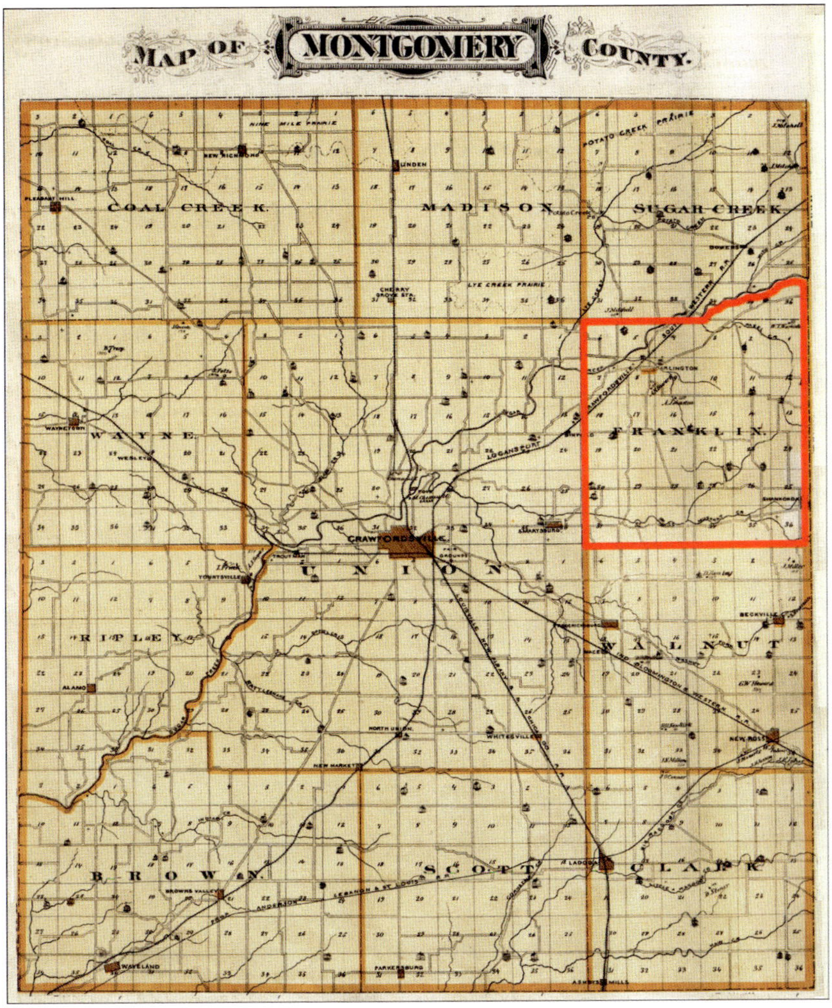

This area was settled as early as 1823, near present-day Darlington. Like Madison Township, Franklin was full of swamps, but was drained by a system of ditches in order to establish a rich farming area. It was said in the late nineteenth century that the physical features of the land had no points of interest, but was unsurpassed in its agricultural possibilities. Sugar Creek was once a major source of water power, and several mills were established here, with the first mill in 1833 about a half-mile downstream from Darlington. Darlington is the main town; Darlington Woods and Shannondale are unincorporated.

COVERED BRIDGE: The Darlington Covered Bridge was built in 1868 as a single span, Howe truss bridge of oak and poplar, and it crosses Sugar Creek just west of Darlington. It was closed to vehicles in 1976, but is still open to pedestrian traffic. The 169-foot bridge was added to the National Register of Historic Places in 1990.

Darlington Armory: The Darlington National Guard Armory was completed in 1937 and served for decades as the center for Darlington's 151st Long Range Surveillance Detachment. The structure's Art Deco style rendered it very distinct. In 2008, the National Guard donated the Armory to the town, and the structure was repurposed as the Darlington Community Center.

DARLINGTON BUSINESS DISTRICT: The nineteenth-century Crawfordsville-Thorntown pike road ran through Darlington, and was originally a corduroy road (made of logs placed perpendicular to the direction of the road) before it was eventually graveled and then later paved. The many businesses along West Main Street in the 1920s have long since disappeared, but modern residents would still recognize many of the structures.

5

Walnut Township

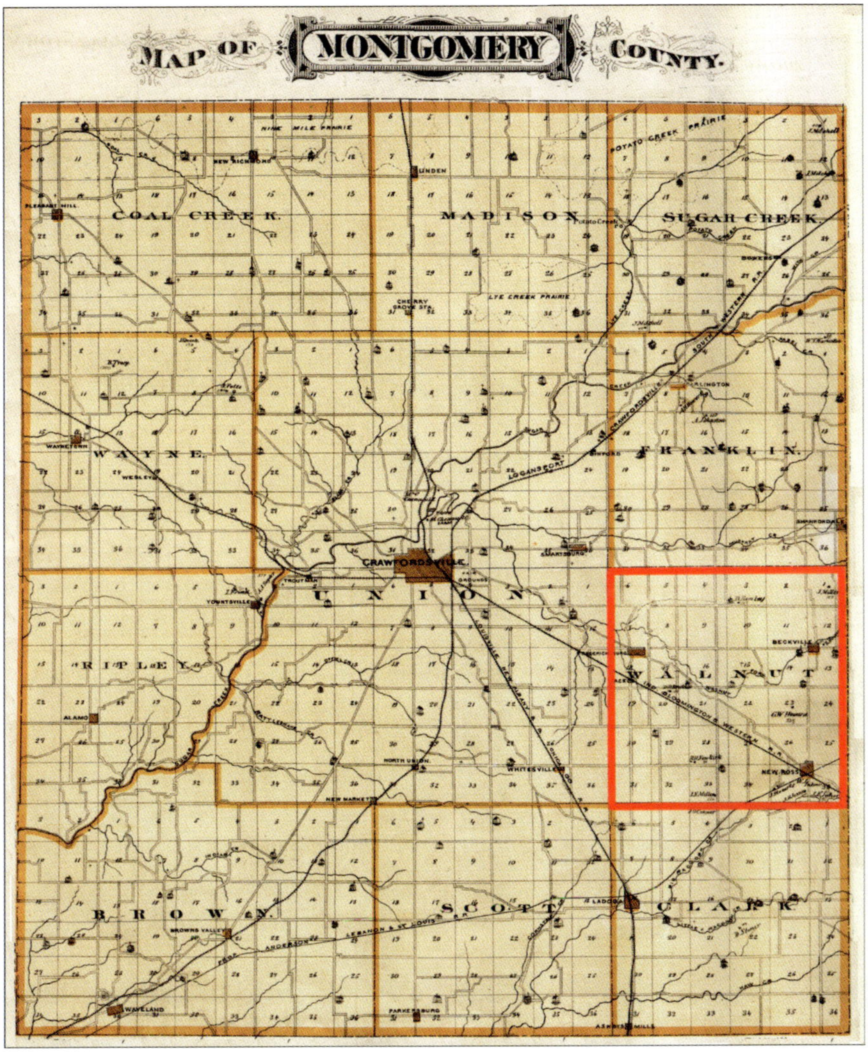

Walnut Township was named after the large tracts of walnut timber growing along what was called Walnut Creek. Walnut is a fairly level section of land that was densely forested before the arrival of settlers around 1824. A post office called the New Ross Post Office was established in Walnut Township by 1837, and when it was moved to what was then called Valley City, the town's name was changed to New Ross. New Ross was incorporated in 1870. Mace and Linnsburg are unincorporated.

New Ross Early School: The first township schools were log constructions, and after some time, several frame buildings were erected. A more substantial structure was built *circa* 1871 on North Street, next to its predecessor. This building was the New Ross-Walnut Township School. No trace of these structures exists today.

TOWNSHIP SCHOOLS: New Ross and Mace both enjoyed a series of schools, and especially handsome was the New Ross Elementary in the early twentieth century. In the 1960s, however, a school consolidation took place in the county; Walnut Elementary School was constructed in 1963 between Mace and New Ross, and became part of the South Montgomery School Corporation. The older schools were eventually demolished.

LINNSBURG AND THE INTERURBAN: At one time, Indiana was crisscrossed with interurban train service, and most of Montgomery County was within easy reach of elsewhere. The track for the Indianapolis, Crawfordsville, and Western Line was laid in the early 1900s, southwest of Mace, with the overhead lines running to Linnsburg. The interurban had tracks that ran parallel to the Big Four railroad.

6

CLARK TOWNSHIP

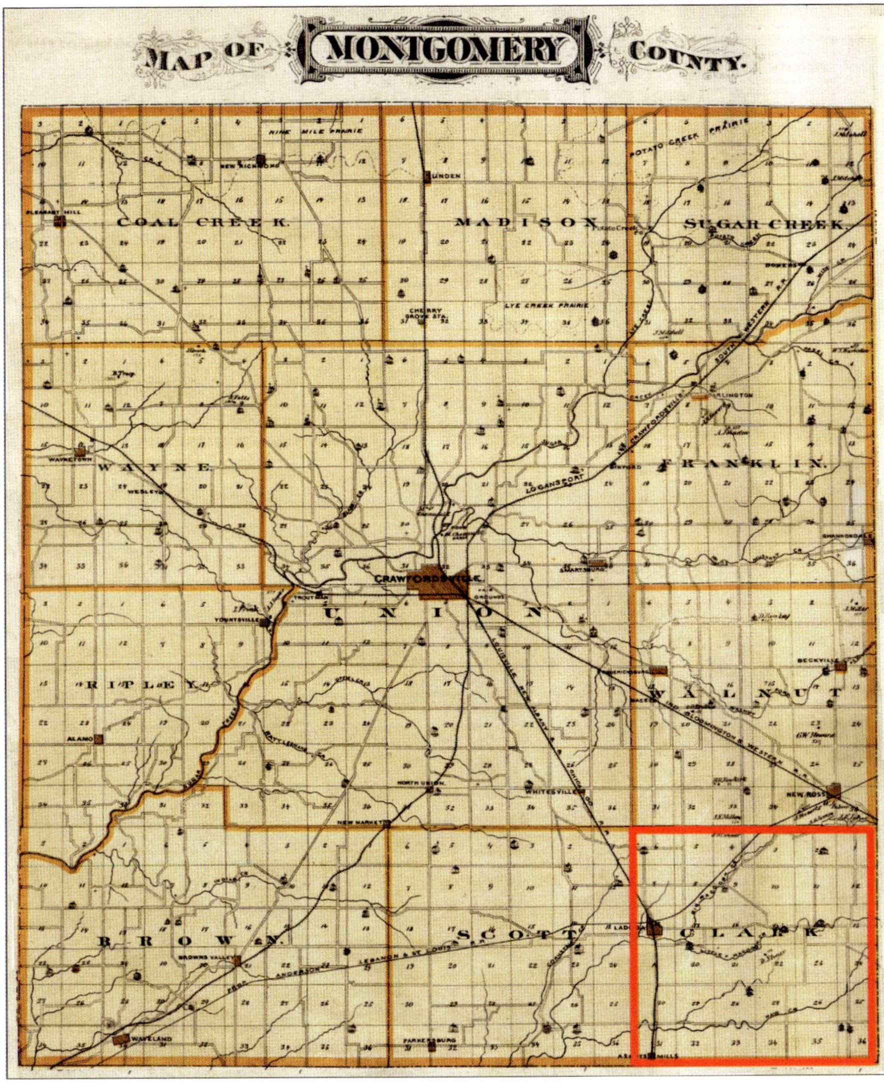

Named after Daniel Clark, an early settler, Clark township (along with neighboring Scott township) was settled after the other townships because of the thick forest growth and the presence of Native American tribes that claimed the area for their hunting grounds. Clark Township was once known as the most heavily forested section of the county. Ladoga is its principal town.

WASHINGTON STREET, LADOGA: Ladoga was laid out in 1836 by John Myers, who invited his friends to help him choose a name for it. He insisted, however, that the name should not end with "ville" or "burg." When no suitable name was suggested, the son of a local blacksmith looked through his atlas and came across a lake now in Russia, Lake Ladoga. By 1890, Ladoga was thriving if still unpaved, and still retains much of its original business district.

MAIN STREET, LADOGA: Ladoga's business district is still its hub, and its Main Street resembles the appearance it held in the late nineteenth and early twentieth century when Ladoga experienced strong economic activity. By 1920, Ladoga had around 1,010 residents. The population was 985 at the 2010 census.

LADOGA NORMAL SCHOOL: Central Indiana Normal College was built in 1878 as a private school specializing in teacher training. By 1889, 594 students were enrolled, but the final class graduated in 1891. It then served in various capacities but eventually fell into disrepair by 1993. Normal Hall was listed on the National Register of Historic Places in 1996, and restoration began the next year to bring it back to its former state.

7

Scott Township

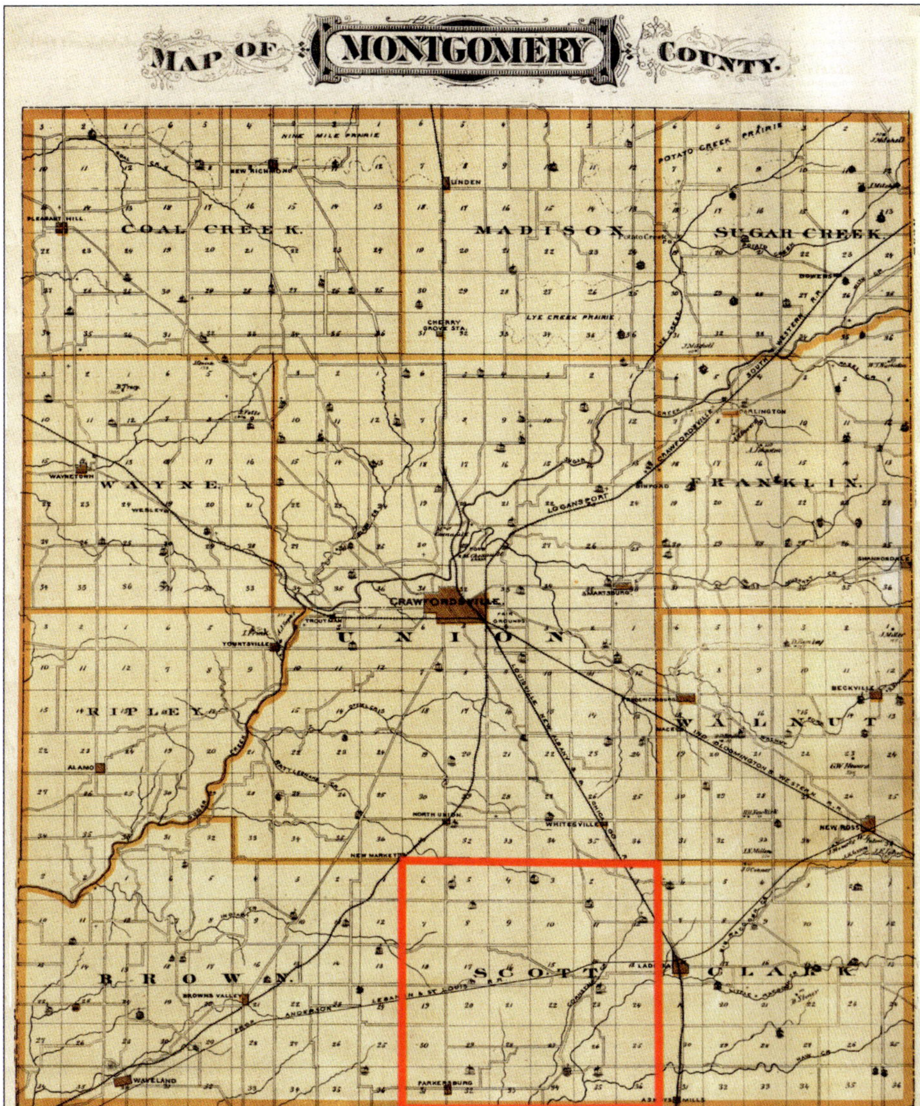

Settlers arrived in the Scott township area as early as 1820, and it was recognized as a very productive region for grazing and general farming thanks to a system of underground drainage that was created in the last decades of the nineteenth century. New Market is the main town; Parkersburg and Lapland are unincorporated.

New Market School Building: In 1898, a brick, six-room New Market School House was completed. It housed elementary school students on the first floor, and high-school students on the second. By 1928, it was considered a fire hazard and replaced by another larger structure, itself replaced with the current New Market Elementary, which still conducts school on the same spot (kindergarten through sixth grades).

Baseball Players: Baseball was an especially popular sport in Montgomery County in the first decades of the twentieth century, and New Market was no exception. The population of the town grew steadily from 119 in 1880 to over 600 by the time of the 2010 census. Organized baseball for youth is still a summer staple on several of New Market's fields.

Parkersburg: Platted in 1837, Parkersburg was once considered the biggest rival to Ladoga, the second-largest community in Montgomery County, but ended up almost disappearing because of the few roads that came through the area. By 1900, the general store and the public spring were the only offerings. A busy U.S. 231 highway rushes modern travelers though this area now, much too late to resurrect the fortunes of the town.

8

Brown Township

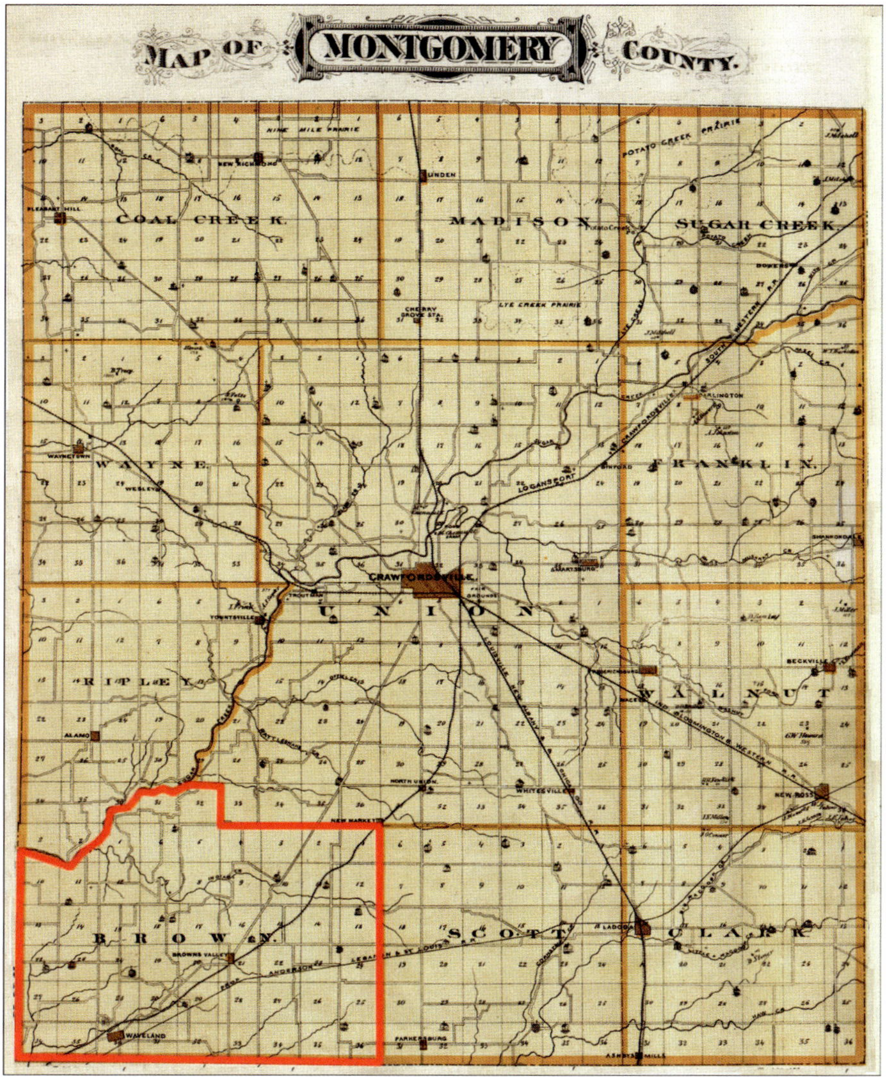

Brown Township attracted settlers after 1822, with the majority arriving from Kentucky. This area was known for its old, dense forests, and it was recognized as a destination because of attractions for sightseeing and exploration. The region is famous for Shades Sate Park, which started out in the late nineteenth century as a resort with an inn. The oldest town in the area is Waveland, laid out by 1835.

Hotel Waveland: The hotel was located on Cross Street at the corner of Howard, where the building still stands. By 1910, the town had grown to 676 inhabitants, and catered often to the travelers to what would later become Shades State Park. However, the population decreased yearly since then and fell to 420 by the 2010 census.

WAVELAND WEST MAIN STREET: The origin of Waveland's name is unknown, but it is assumed to refer to the gently rolling hills of the area that resemble the waves of the ocean. In the early 1890s, a town ordinance was passed that required every property owner to plant trees. Main street is less shady today, but still very much residential.

THE SHADES: Touching upon areas in Montgomery, Parke, and Fountain counties, the wooded resort area known as the Shades was bought in the 1930s by Joseph Frisz. Frisz purchased the land in order to protect it, and his heirs sold his holdings in 1947 to the "Save the Shades" holding company. The annual amount of visitors since 2015 has surpassed 100,000.

9

Ripley Township

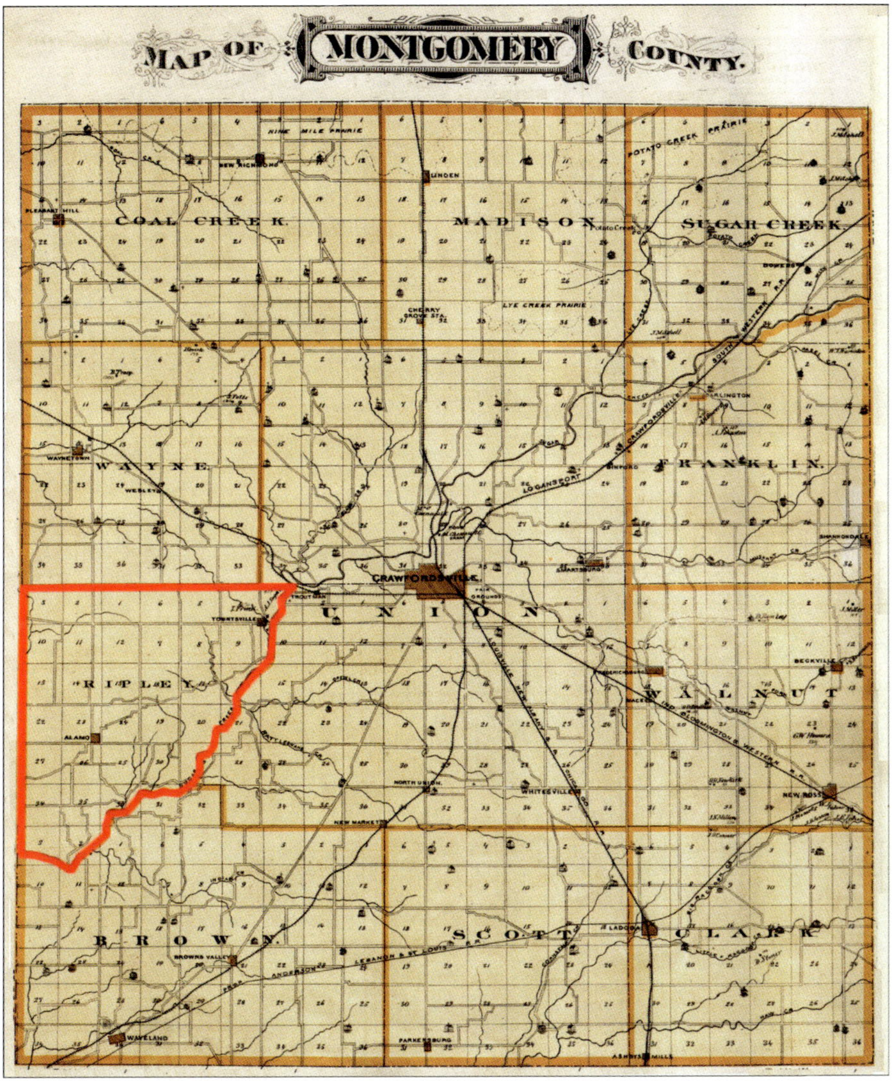

The first cabin erected in Ripley township is reputed to have been in 1820, and the area was densely forested. It is the smallest township in the county, and the only without railroads. Five mills were operating in 1880, and timber was already becoming scarce. Alamo is its main town, named after the famous Alamo Mission in San Antonio, Texas. Unincorporated communities include Deer Mill, Hibernia, and Yountsville.

ALAMO HIGH SCHOOL BASKETBALL: The 1919-1920 Basketball team posed outside the Alamo High School building, completed in 1913, but no longer existing. In 1941, the Alamo Gymnasium was built by the WPA; it was saved after the school building was demolished, but has since been neglected. Alamo's population fell from 209 in 1910 to 66 by 2010.

YOUNTSVILLE COVERED BRIDGE: Built in 1858 as a burr type, double-tunnel bridge, the Yountsville Covered Bridge was perched 40 feet above Sugar Creek, and nearly 200 feet long. The deteriorating bridge was dismantled in 1948 and replaced by a concrete span that, itself, had to undergo extensive repairs in 1979 and again in 2019 to ensure its safety.

YOUNT'S WOOLEN MILL: A series of mills was constructed starting in the 1830s alongside Sugar Creek. Eventually a large brick mill was erected in 1864 and served until 1905, providing work and supplies for the area. The mill was listed on the National Register of Historic Places in 1989, and one building was restored as an inn—the original boarding house for young working women at the mill during the mid-nineteenth century.

10

Wayne Township

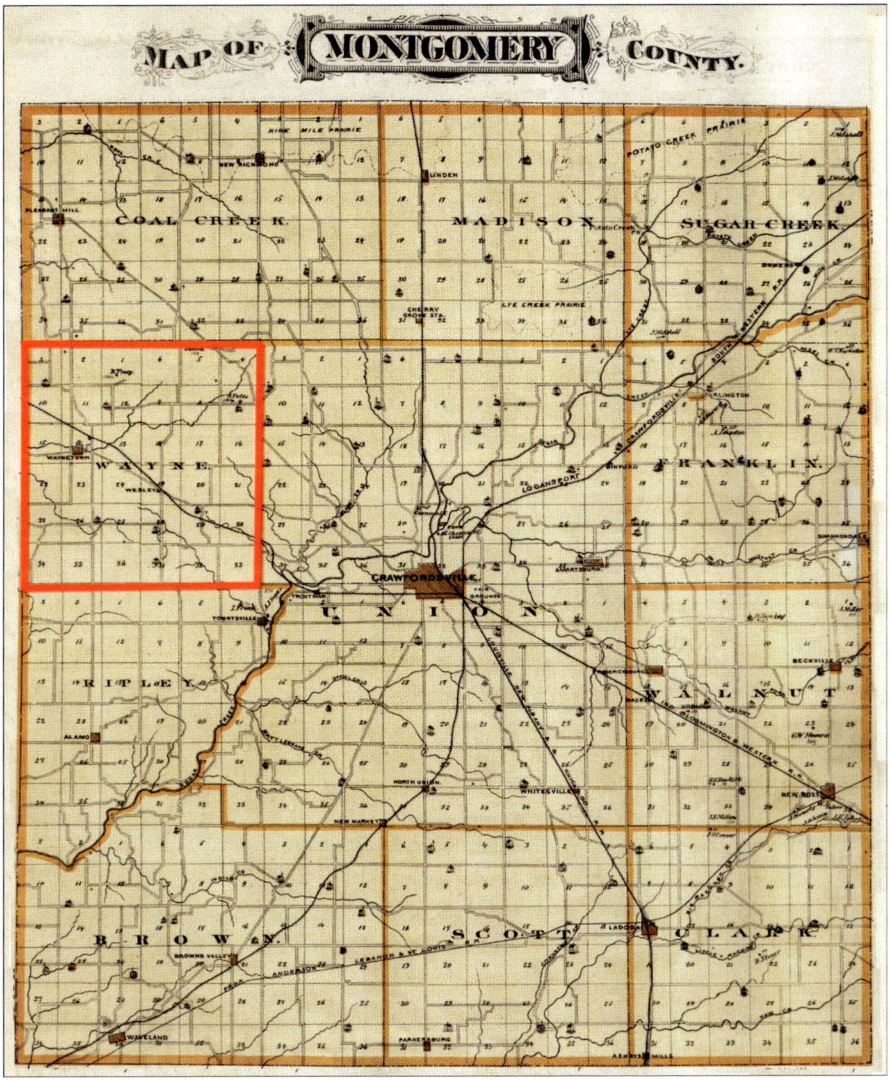

The first European settlers arrived in this area of the county in 1823, turning its forests to farmland. Perhaps its most famous citizen was William Bratton (1778-1841), a member of the 1804 Lewis and Clark Expedition. Bratton held various and township offices, and is buried in Old Pioneer Cemetery within Waynetown, which is the principal town; Wesley is unincorporated.

WASHINGTON STREET, WAYNETOWN: By the end of the nineteenth century, Waynetown had grown to 757 residents and was flourishing with numerous businesses. It saw its first electric lights in 1897, when the arc lights were installed. Washington Street eventually became U.S. Highway 136, and the town continued to grow; the population was 958 at the 2010 census.

BRIDGE AND EXCHANGE MILLS, WAYNETOWN: Coal Creek runs through Waynetown, and was a more important and even volatile tributary of Sugar Creek, the main water source running across the county. There were numerous sawmills in the township because of the quantity of timber to be found. Waynetown was even a pork-packing center with a packing house near the creek, whose product was hauled to Covington by wagon and shipped to New Orleans in flat boats.

WESLEY METHODIST EPISCOPAL CHURCH: The church was constructed in 1901 and is still located on State Road 136 West. It stands on the opposite hill from the Wesley School (or Wesley Academy), which was built in 1910. The church has continued to hold occasional services. The church cemetery is still in use, and is located behind the church building.

11
Union Township

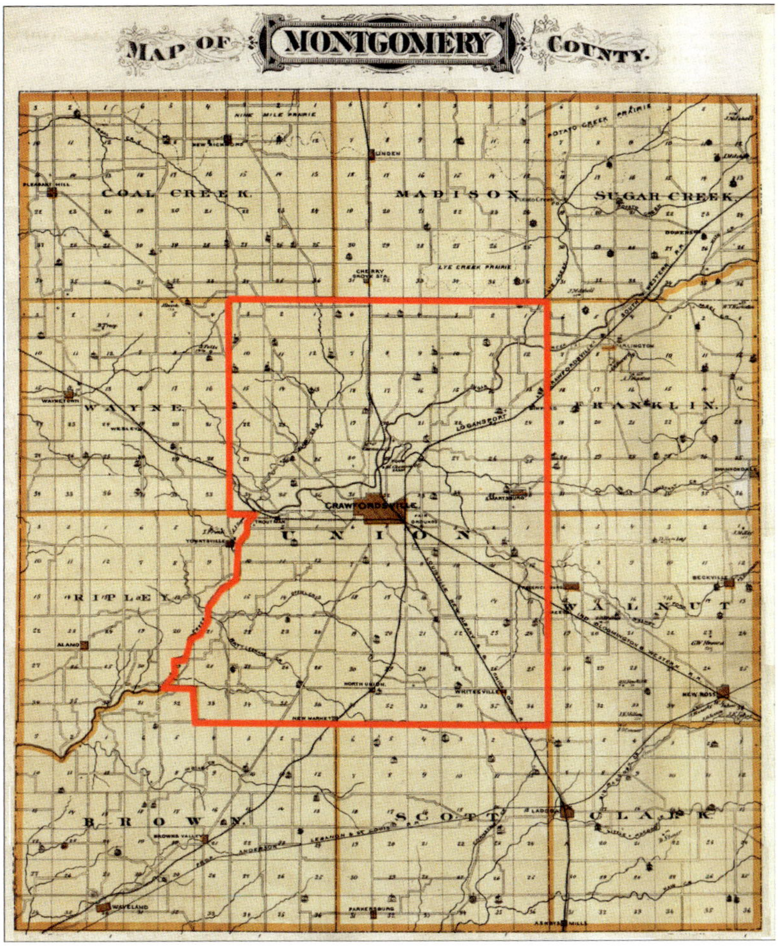

Union Township is the largest in the county, and the most populous (as of 2010, 24,587 residents), with Crawfordsville as the county seat. In 1823, Congress moved the land office from Terre Haute to Crawfordsville, laid out by Major Ambrose Whitlock, who reputedly named the town after his friend, Colonel William Crawford. The location of Crawfordsville enabled its steady growth; the town was supposedly located near one of the Native American trails that crossed Ohio, Indiana, and Illinois—and was therefore a major route for immigrants moving from east into the western regions. Only during the 1970s and 1980s did Crawfordsville experience a decline in population. Otherwise, the town has grown steadily from 1,327 in 1840 to 15,915 by 2010.

MONTGOMERY COUNTY COURTHOUSE: The original county courthouse in Crawfordsville was constructed around 1824 and was a two-story building, twenty-six feet long by twenty feet wide, all of hewed twelve-inch logs. Built for a contract price of $295, this rough structure was replaced in 1833 by a brick structure forty-five feet square at a cost of $3,420. At this time, Crawfordsville had less than 1,000 residents.

MONTGOMERY COUNTY COURTHOUSE CEREMONY: A large crowd estimated to be more than 6,000 witnessed the cornerstone laying for the third Montgomery County Courthouse on May 6, 1875. This structure, completed two years later, was constructed of Berea sandstone, brick, and iron at a cost of $150,000. General Lew Wallace was scheduled to speak at the outdoor cornerstone ceremony, but rain forced him into a nearby hall where he finished his delivery.

LEW WALLACE STUDY: Among his many accomplishments, General Lew Wallace is perhaps most well known as the author of the novel *Ben-Hur*, published in 1880. Wallace designed and built his personal study in 1895, on the spot where he wrote his famous novel. This study is preserved by the General Lew Wallace Study & Museum.

LANE PLACE: This distinguished home in Crawfordsville was begun in 1845 by Senator Henry Smith Lane (1811-1881) and his wife, Joanna Elston Lane (1826-1914). Helen Elston Smith, Joanna's niece, inherited the home and eventually deeded the house and its contents in 1931 to the Montgomery County Historical Society, which has maintained it as a museum ever since. Most of the furnishings are original to the house or once belonged to the Elston Family.

Y.M.C.A. GYM: The Y.M.C.A. building in Crawfordsville, built in 1888, was situated near Crawfordsville's busy corner of Washington Street and West Main Street. Its gym on the second floor witnessed the first organized basketball game to be played in Indiana on March 16, 1894. Nothing remains of the structure today, but it is commemorated with a historical marker proclaiming this area as the cradle of basketball.

DOWNTOWN CRAWFORDSVILLE: Looking north along the Washington Street business district in 1913 reveals the extent of the town's busy activity, including an interurban car, ready to depart from the Ben Hur Terminal Station located just north of the courthouse. By the 1950s, the interurban had been gone for decades, but business still thrived. Castle Hall (demolished 1999) is seen on Market Street in both photos, in the distance. This block is now a parking area for the courthouse.

LOCAL MILK DELIVERY: The Sanitary Milk Depot was located at 118-120 West Pike Street, and the milk delivery wagon was still horse-powered in the late 1920s. This corner was later turned into apartments and businesses but burned down in May 2007, and it remained an empty lot until Crawfordsville was designated a Stellar Community in 2015; part of the grant was dedicated to creating a pocket park, completed in 2019.

MARKET AND WASHINGTON STREETS: Willis Grocery was located in the early twentieth century on the busy southwest corner of Market and Washington Streets (U.S. 231) in Crawfordsville. This corner has seen since a variety of businesses. In 1922, the store become Francis & Mount, a feed store, and in 2019 became a restaurant by the same name.

"Old" Crawfordsville Post Office: The town's original post office was established in 1823, located in various places, but in 1906 a new building was constructed on the northwest corner of Main and Water Streets. It was replaced in 1941 with a structure on the northeast corner of Main and Water Streets, where it still serves at the time of writing.

"NEW" CRAWFORDSVILLE POST OFFICE: To prepare East Main Street for the new post office in 1941, the Community House (302 East Main) and a few others were removed. The Community House and cafeteria served meals in the community. The Community House was founded by Dr. Martha Griffith, who also helped to organize the Carnegie Library in 1897.

Washington Street Activity: Except for the business occupying the buildings, this section of Washington Street has changed little since the late nineteenth century. Although it is now the main artery through Crawfordsville, this thoroughfare was calm enough for a car display *circa* 1910. Now the traffic on U.S. 231 makes it difficult to imagine any stationary activity on this busy thoroughfare, and standing in the road for a closer photograph is not to be attempted.

MOONSHINING SHUT DOWN: On June 30, 1923, local authorities raided a still at Waynetown and brought its parts back to Crawfordsville. The group posed in the 100 block North Green Street for a publicity photo, and the newspaper headline declared "Moonshiners out of Biz." At the end of the block is the still recognizable Otto Schlemmer building (built 1854) that was listed on the National Register of Historic Places in 1985.

Crawfordsville Business District: The building on the southeast corner of Washington and Main Streets (pictured across from the courthouse on the following page) has been a favored spot for several businesses throughout the years. In the nineteenth century, it was a clothing and dry goods store; more recently, it has been a bank, a jewelry store, and at the time of writing, a restaurant. The vault at the back of the building is still used as a dining area.

BUSY INTERSECTION: The crossing of the two busiest streets in Crawfordsville, looking east on Main Street, across Washington Street. The courthouse (seen on the left) and the commercial building (seen on the right) have existed since the last quarter of the nineteenth century and have witnessed most of the town's public gatherings and parades.

Crawfordsville Library Children's Room: Until an adjacent building was purchased in 1979, and a remodeling project permitted the expansion of the library, the children's room was a large part of the original Carnegie library plan. This room then became the library reference area, and when remodeled for the Carnegie Museum of Montgomery County after 2005, the space became the museum's Business & Industry Gallery.

BEN-HUR STATION: The interurban station stood just north of the Crawfordsville courthouse on Washington Street, as seen in 1911. The Indianapolis, Crawfordsville and Western Traction Company created the Ben Hur Route (in honor of Lew Wallace's novel). Indianapolis was a popular destination; tracks ran south on Washington Street, turning east on Wabash Avenue to Grace Avenue, and then ran south before turning again east to Indianapolis.

LOCAL TRANSPORT: A large stagecoach is parked in front of 102 West Main Street in Crawfordsville, *circa* 1903, with ten people on the top of the stagecoach, and four people visible inside. The flyers on the stagecoach mention a "Base Ball Game." The second-floor door and stairwell have been removed, but much of the facade has remained unchanged.

CRAWFORD HOTEL CONSTRUCTION: Thomas Clark, a local tailor, stood for a photo *circa* 1899 in the intersection of Green and East Main Streets, in front of the lot where the Crawford Hotel was being constructed. An advertisement for Tafel Beer is painted on the side of one building, soon to be hidden by the hotel. The Crawford Hotel would be the most elegant hotel in town and a favorite for visiting celebrities.

CRAWFORD HOTEL DESTRUCTION: The Crawford Hotel had nearly 100 rooms and many modern amenities for its time, and several businesses were located on the street-level floor. However, it fell into a great amount of disrepair by the 1970s and was eventually demolished in 1974. The advertisement for Tafel beer was rediscovered and recreated when Crawfordsville constructed the Canine Plaza, which occupied the spot in 2003.

CRAWFORDSVILLE STREET SCENE: A souvenir card sold in Crawfordsville *circa* 1900 shows the intersection of Washington and Main Streets, with the courthouse as its focal point. Interurban tracks can be seen running down both bricked streets, and a lone automobile appears parked near the courthouse on Main Street, but the evidence in the streets of horses for transport is still apparent.

MASONIC TEMPLE: A street view *circa* 1905 shows the intersection of Washington and Wabash Streets, with the Masonic Temple standing in on the northwest corner. The cornerstone of the temple was laid in 1901, and in 1904, member Lew Wallace participated in the dedication, leading the parade. Interurban tracks run along Washington Street and curve east onto Wabash Avenue on their way to Indianapolis and beyond.

WASHINGTON STREET: The intersection of Washington and Market Streets in downtown Crawfordsville in the early 1940s was a busy business district, including the long-time favorite Coney Island Shop. The Montgomery County Courthouse is seen in the background, before its tower was removed in 1941. This block is now gone, but the courthouse tower was reconstructed in 2018.

SPANISH-AMERICAN WAR: The Spanish-American War was an armed conflict in 1898 between Spain and the United States, and Montgomery County citizens served in large numbers. At least 150 veterans of the war are buried in county cemeteries. This largely forgotten conflict is still honored by the Spanish-American War memorial, located in Milligan Park. It commemorates Company M, 158th Indiana Voluntary Infantry's involvement in the war.

METHODIST EPISCOPAL CHURCH: The Crawfordsville Methodist Episcopal Church was built 1855 on the corner of Wabash Avenue and Water Streets. This Gothic-style church was razed in 1886, and its successor was again replaced with another building in 1976. It continues to face the Lane Place, whose iron fence runs along Wabash Avenue and Water Street.

CRAWFORDSVILLE JOURNAL: The *Crawfordsville Journal* building was constructed in 1892 in the 100 block of South Green Street. At a reunion held in 1897, former employees posed in front of the building. The *Crawfordsville Journal* merged with the *Crawfordsville Review* in 1929 and relocated eventually to North Green Street.

STRAND THEATER: The Strand Theater (originally the Music Hall) was located on South Green Street just before the intersection with Pike Street. It served Crawfordsville for decades as an auditorium and eventually movie house, very popular in the 1930s. The movies advertised in the modern picture date the photo to 1993. The theater was damaged in a windstorm in 1999 and a wall collapsed. The demolition took place later that same year.

DOWNTOWN FIRE: A large section of downtown Crawfordsville went up in flames on January 10, 1933. The intersection of Green and East Main Streets, which held Goodman's Department Store (formerly Bischof's Big Store), smoldered for days. More than a dozen businesses were destroyed or damaged, including the Schultz Book Store, the Central Drug Store, and the J. C. Penny Store.

CITY BUILDING: The Crawfordsville City Municipal Building was constructed in 1933 on the corner of Water and Pike Streets; it housed not only the fire department, but also the police department as well as various other offices, including that of mayor. The police department relocated to a new building at the turn of the twenty-first century, but the Municipal Building, shown in the early 1950s, remains at the time of writing much as it was.

INTERURBAN TRACK CONSTRUCTION: In the early years of the twentieth century, Crawfordsville joined the interurban system that was connecting much of the state. Tracks ran down several town streets, including what is now U.S. 231, just north of the Market Street intersection. The courthouse tower can be seen on the left. The interurban eventually gave way to the automobile, and the last train left Crawfordsville for Indianapolis on October 31, 1930.

MILLIGAN PARK: In 1911, Harry Milligan donated land in memory of his father for a city park. Milligan Park opened a few years later and still resembles in many areas the initial layout, pictured in the *circa* 1920 postcard. The band stand used in the early days of the park for Sunday concerts remains, unused, in the same location, and the original horseshoe pits have not been moved in spite of newer additions such as a skate park and a Frisbee golf course.

CULVER UNION HOSPITAL: The original Culver Union hospital was built in 1902 at 308 Binford Street, but was replaced in 1929 by the newer structure advertised in this color postcard. The building was abandoned in 1984 when a new hospital was constructed north of Crawfordsville's business district on U.S. 231. After years of neglect, the 1929 structure was restored to become the Historic Whitlock Place in 2016.

EAST MAIN STREET: Main Street had long been a favored residential section of the town, as seen in this 1911 postcard. Interurban tracks ran down Main Street on their destination further east to Indianapolis and beyond. At the time of writing, the homes remain much the same as they were more than a century ago.

MAIN AND WASHINGTON STREETS: In 1865, the intersection of Main Street where it crossed Washington Street featured a four-story brick structure, erected in 1836, that held the offices of the *Crawfordsville Journal*. To the right appears a fence and hitching post that bordered what was then the courthouse (the present-day courthouse was built on that site in 1876). The same scene is shown in the early 1900s, as a parade marches east on Main Street.

BEN HUR BUILDING: The Ben Hur Life Association, a fraternal benefit society founded in 1894, erected a building on the corner of Water and Main Streets. The construction photo was taken on September 7, 1911. The building was modernized in 1940 and remained in service until the 1990s when it was vacated. Several plans have been made to restore this local landmark.

Main and Green Streets: Dr. Elliot Detchon stood (far left) in front of his drugstore around 1895, located on the southwest corner of East Main and South Green Streets. The family grew rich through the "proprietary medicine" business. The same corner later held the Louis Bischof Big Store and then Goodman's Department Store, which burned to the ground in 1933. This much-changed corner should be familiar to all local residents.

Main Street: A 1913 postcard shows the north side of Main Street, looking west toward the Montgomery County Courthouse. The tall building on the right was the Crawford Hotel, a landmark until its destruction in the late 1970s. Tracks for the interurban train are visible in the street, shared with automobiles and horses.

MID-NINETEENTH CENTURY DOWNTOWN: Looking north on Green Street in 1865, from the corner of Main Street, reveals the township trustee's office and a dry goods store with a sign for groceries, boots, shoes, and clothing. The corner became the location for the Crawford Hotel and was eventually made into the Canine Plaza, well after the hotel was demolished in 1974.

STUDENT GATHERING: A large group of young men and women stand at the northeast corner of Green and Jefferson Streets, just in front of the Crawfordsville High School building that opened in 1911 and which served as a school until 1993. In 2000, the former school building was converted to a multi-use facility of offices, residential housing, and a fitness center.

HOSE SCHOOL: The Laura G. Hose Elementary School of Crawfordsville (800 Fairview Ave.) was opened in 1954, and several additions were completed over the next three decades. In 1999, the school was completely remodeled. At the time of writing it contains a kindergarten and first grade population of more than 400 students bussed from throughout the school corporation.

WILLSON SCHOOL: Erected in 1897 on the property of Laura Willson, this school faced East Wabash Avenue in Crawfordsville. Seen here in 1911, Willson School contained six grades and 356 students. In 1964, this structure was demolished and replaced by a newer school named Anna Willson School; Anna was the granddaughter of Laura, and popular teacher in the early 1900s. The entrance now faces toward Jefferson Street, and at the time of writing is a Pre-K school.

TUTTLE SCHOOL: The Tuttle building opened in 1906 between South Elm Street and Wallace Avenue, just south of the Big Four railroad tracks. In 1961, it was replaced with Joseph F. Tuttle Jr. High for grades 7-9, but in 1986 it became a school for grades 6-8 and was renamed Tuttle Middle School. It was completely redone and expanded in stages starting in 2013 to become Crawfordsville Middle School.

GRADE SCHOOL STUDENTS: Mills School students posed for a class photograph in 1935, as did their fourth-grade counterparts at John Beard Elementary School in 1961. Today, Mills and Beard still stand but are no longer used as elementary schools. Remaining Crawfordsville schools include Laura G. Hose Elementary (grades K-1), Meredith Nicholson Elementary (grades 2-3), and Mollie B. Hoover Elementary (grades 4-5).

Caleb Mills Elementary School: In 1909, Mills School stood facing West Main Street, along which ran tracks for the interurban system. The school was replaced in the 1960s, with its entrance on Pike Street. Mills remained in service as a school into the current century before it was repurposed; it eventually became the new Crawfordsville home of the Montgomery County Youth Services Bureau in 2019.

COLLEGE HILL: Wabash Avenue runs west past Wabash College through a part of town named College Hill because of its incline. The steps leading to the Wabash arboretum did not change much after the appearance of this 1910 postcard, and this scene would be familiar to generations of Wabash students. But in mid-2019 the college began to replace this entrance with a newer gateway as part of the Crawfordsville Downtown Loop Trail project.

Water Street: Water Street contains some of the oldest homes in Crawfordsville and was a favored residential district. The street was named for a ravine that was located near its north end, and in the early days of Crawfordsville Water Street was considered the eastern boundary of the town limits (bounded by North Street, Grant Avenue to the west, and Wabash Avenue to the south).

HARRY S. TRUMAN: During his 1948 whistle-stop campaign for the presidency, Harry Truman's train stopped briefly in Crawfordsville (October 12, 1948) on the tracks that crossed Washington Street. He drew a sizeable crowd even though the town voted 3,373 to 2,230 in favor of his Republican opponent, Thomas Dewey. The tracks are no longer very active, and the traffic of a busy U.S. 231 would be difficult to detour for a similar event today.

CRAWFORDSVILLE HIGH SCHOOL: The "new" Crawfordsville High School opened on September 4, 1911, incorporating the school that was located on the same spot (and whose tower can still be seen in the background). Many generations of students went through these halls, and Crawfordsville's 100th graduating class received diplomas in this same building in 1976. The school served until 1993 and was added to the National Register of Historic Places in 2003.

UNITED BRETHREN CHURCH: This denomination had several churches in the county, and the Crawfordsville edifice was constructed in 1906 on the corner of East Main and Oak, along with a frame parsonage, at a cost of $20,000. On July 1, 1928, some of the congregation posed outside the church, and the structure appears much the same neatly a century later. The church has since become United Methodist.

ORIGINAL SITE OF WABASH COLLEGE: On June 12, 1916, the faculty, trustees, and friends of Wabash College gathered at the corner of Lane Avenue and Blair Street in Crawfordsville to commemorate the location of the college's first building. The monument was a tablet of Vermont granite placed on a concrete base, and it remains in this spot where the town constructed a cement curb just in time for the ceremony.